VIGILANT

HOW TO SEE WHAT OTHERS MISS

A SYSTEM FOR YOUR PERSONAL SAFETY, SUCCESS, AND OTHER LIFE SECRETS

Suzanne Cruz

This book is dedicated to:
Those who embrace life's challenges, keep growing and who always seek truth. By doing so strengthen themselves, their families and communities. Thank you for enhancing all our lives.

MURPHY'S LAWS
OF COMBAT

1. If the enemy is in range, so are you.
2. Incoming fire has the right of way.
3. Don't look conspicuous, it draws fire.
4. There is always a way.
5. The easy way is always mined.
6. Try to look unimportant, they may be low on ammo.
7. Professionals are predictable, it's the amateurs that are dangerous.
8. The enemy invariably attacks on two occasions:
   a. When you're ready for them.
   b. When you are not ready for them.
9. Teamwork is essential, it gives them someone else to shoot at.
10. The enemy diversion you have been ignoring will be the main attack.
11. If your attack is going well, you have walked into an ambush.
12. Never draw fire, it irritates everyone around you.
13. Anything you do can get you shot, including nothing.

CONTENTS

INTRODUCTION

My cousin warned me not to, but I took him home anyway. He was a young adult dog my girlfriend was not allowed to keep for various reasons. I talked myself into him, after all something this cute could not be left for someone else to have, right? And who cares if I was still living at home, I was almost an adult and able to make my own decisions, right?

I immediately imagined me and my dog spending many quality years together. Romping through the grass, perfectly trained and playing fetch, roll over, eagerly jumping into my arms and licking me all over the face. Like the Sphinx of Egypt, he would sit regally on the front porch and wait for me to get home in the evenings. Well, that is how I imagined it.

Not too long after I got the dog home, it pooped on the carpet then ate its own poop, ran away when I called it, dug up all my mom's roses and when I was away, chewed on the molding around the door frames. About four hundred dollars later in damages and vet bills, I realized I had a lot to learn about dogs. In fact, I had a great epiphany about life, that if I wanted to get ahead in anything I would need to mitigate the obstacles, and part of that was not creating my own obstacles!

Needless to say, my mother would have none of this chaos in HER home. I eventually was made to give the dog away and did not get another one till 30 years later. Older, wiser and with a home of my own, I was now much better equipped to put in the time, and attention to get the dog of my dreams.

———❧❧❧———

Looking back, I clearly wanted to believe what I wanted to believe, my mind and emotions were biased to what I wanted. I was willing to ignore my inner sense that told me getting a dog was a stupid idea! I disregard my friend's warnings, my mom's feelings, threw caution to the wind and just did it and I paid the price.

Sometimes people's emotions over-ride their brains, we just don't think; or we seek out only information that agrees with what we think, *Cognitive Bias.* Establishing this sort of selective thinking habit dangerously spreads to different areas like, finances, political views, history, or the character flaw of a close relationship, and you have a recipe for disaster. Now factor in when other people deliberately keep information from us, then the game of life just got even harder!

IN ORDER TO SEE WHAT OTHER PEOPLE MISS, we must first ask ourselves if we are honestly seeking the absolute truth every moment of the day.

~The Matrix filmed in 1999, is a futuristic story about the pains it takes to get to the truth. If you have not seen it, it depicts a dystopian future in which people live in a world that is not real. The hero Neo, discovers the truth, that humans are being used, and living in a state of suspended animation. He gets busy attempting to set people free; however, a surprising turn of events reveals that many people decide they want to stay in the matrix, the lie. The audience is left with the now pop culture question, "do you want the red pill or the blue pill?"

The Matrix is actually a modern version of The Allegory of the Cave. In 380 B.C., philosopher Plato realized human's tendency to live a dualistic life, one in truth and one in a lie. American essayist Ralph Waldo Emerson once declared, "Burn all the libraries for their value is in this one book." It is superb reading for philosophers and leaders alike. The Allegory of the Cave, a beautiful metaphor, still powerful and relevant today.

As Socrates tells Glaucon the allegory (the tale) of the cave, the reader discovers universal truths about humanity. The resistance to change, the resistance to truth, protection of the ego, cognitive bias, retribution and anger for being shown the truth and finally two outcomes, either there are people who want to continue to believe in untruth to their detriment and those that realize they were wrong and can adapt and change to their benefit.

Summary:

Socrates asks Glaucon to imagine a cave, in which prisoners are kept. They have been in the cave their whole lives, sitting chained and unmoving in chairs which face a wall where shadows are cast. The prisoners believe that the shadows are reality, what life is. These poor fellows believe that this is the world for years on end until one day one of the prisoners is set free, and notices that it's all a lie, that in fact the shadows were not real at all, but only shadows of the real things behind them. Socrates goes on to say that if that freed prisoner were to go up to the real world he or she would find the truth and after learning of the reality of the world, his first inclination would be to euphorically sing the truth. However, the prisoner stops himself realizing that they would accuse him of being deranged and probably beat him up (the first haters). The freed prisoner now faces a dilemma: to attempt to enlighten the others in the cave, anyway, and face the retribution, or go up to the light and live in truth by himself.

Imagine now if one of the prisoners had not been forcibly shown the light, but due to her own vigilance had broken free, walked past the shadows of half-truths, group think, popular culture, fake news and indoctrination, thereby transcending what is right in front of her face, moving into a higher world which is more intelligible and more fully real.

—ουο—

I wrote this book because I spent most of my young life saying, "why didn't someone tell me?" and then in my adult life, listening to other people say the very same thing. Knowledge, combined with experience led me to wisdom and what I learned is that very same habits we develop for personal safety are the very same habits of the foundations for success. Now able to differentiate between the bad fear that holds you back from the good fear that keeps you safe, I was unleashed to experience true life successes without unnecessary threats. I am sharing this information with you. You're about to accelerate your learning curve. I am so excited for you to take on the world.

CHAPTER 1

WHAT IT MEANS TO BE VIGILANT

In your life journey, did you ever struggle with a concept that didn't seem complete? You were missing a key piece of it; a small amount of information from which everything hinged? It was like an itch that you couldn't scratch; an item you couldn't put your finger on. The whole thing did not make sense, and then suddenly you got that last bit that made you understand. Finding the answer made you breathe better; everything was now more lucid.

Looking back, you might have thought to yourself, "Man, the struggle to get to the truth, to find clarity was more of an issue than the issue itself!" It was such a hassle to get to the truth that you resolved to pay more attention; to be vigilant.

Then with these new set of eyes something else happened. You started to examine other things in your life and thought, "was I not working with the whole truth all along? The whole time my cheating boyfriend was a cheat? That class I paid for was telling me what to think rather that how to think.

VIGILANCE PAYS OFF

It gives us clarity, and well, being pissed off for discovering all the things we missed; but clarity non-the less. From this point we can breathe better, see better, stand better and make sounder decisions. Operating from this position of strength, you can strategize a plan of action that is ten times more likely to work.

The older we get the more we apply vigilance to our lives. When we are younger we are not so vigilant for two reasons: One, the world is new and fun and we are trusting. Two, we can afford to be a little careless because our parents have our back.

Later in life as we enter the world, the onus is on us to pay attention. We learn quickly the consequences of not being vigilant. Failure to stay on top of things means we risk losing them:

- Not being vigilant with exercise means becoming unfit.
- Not being vigilant with fact finding means we don't always have the truth, costing us time and money.
- Not being vigilant about our individuality and falling into group-think results in loss of our own creativity, our own decision making abilities and we become blinded to truths in order to get along.
- Not being vigilant about our driving, results in accidents.
- Not being vigilant taking the time to secure our valuables results in costly theft of those items.

It helps us discern

There is an old Chinese saying, "if you want to know what water is don't ask a fish." The reason you would not ask a fish is because the fish is in the water, they do not know what it is to be out of the water. This is the way it is with the crowd or popular culture, *if you want to see what other people miss you must stand back from the crowd* and look, really look, and be honest with yourself about what you see, then ask yourself some honest questions.

It helps us accept change

Vigilance will tell us what is going on. The next step is to move, to do something about it. Change is in the wind. Change becomes necessary when a situation gets so uncomfortable that the discomfort caused by doing something about it causes less pain than doing nothing. However, many people do not like change because they are not willing to put in the work, because it's uncomfortable. Discomfort and unfamiliarity is why work places resist change, families resist change and breaking with toxic friends is so difficult for many.

Only two things will spawn change or self-improvement: One, either a person is sick of being at a disadvantage; or two, they have seen that an ounce of prevention is worth a pound of cure. But in either case, knowledge must go in the brain to create an action plan. Lack of information has a tremendous amount to do with paralysis in the decision-making process.

It gives us a thirst for knowledge

With knowledge, the information is now placed in your brain, and with repetition, fear becomes confidence, difficult becomes easy, incompetent becomes competent. Practicing evading threats and spotting opportunities is a movement we repeat over and over again throughout our lives. It's the process and challenge that gives life meaning, that prevents boredom, burnout and depression. It's good for you. It builds healthy self-esteem, which prevents unhealthy addictions and destructive behavior. Gaining new competence in any skill, such as _artfully navigating difficult situations_ and people, automatically _enhances your confidence_ in all other areas. In short, you are going to find the ability to craft effective ways to be a major asset personally, for your family and for the people you work with every day.

It helps us to see more clearly

The duality of being vigilant for threats is that you see beauty better as well and experience joy. You become a person who sees the glass as half full instead of half empty. You become more confident and joyful. Joy is quite different from simple happiness. Happiness is relative and fleeting, joy is something different. It allows you to expect adversity, yet see it as a challenge, to welcome reasonable difficulties as a fun puzzle.

CHAPTER 2

ALL TYPES OF AWARENESS: 👀

Awareness is your vital first step in seeing what others miss. In a world driven to distraction with electronic devices shoved in our faces from phones to T.V monitors at the gas pump, this skill is becoming lost. Safety nor Success is possible without a healthy dose of awareness. Being conscious of the tools and facts we need to function in life allow us to make the best choices. Making sensible choices about our health, where we work, crossing the street unmolested, navigating traffic, relationships and our finances, all fare better when we are aware.

In today's overly-litigious society, it is imperative that we be not only aware of where we are going, but others. In our surroundings, situations, and work relationships; and who we allow into our close inner circles, it all requires that we listen and pay attention.

■ MY STORY

Many years back on a trip to the circus, my seven-year-old son was over the moon with joy, chatter, and excitement. In fact, he was so excited, that as we walked from the parking lot to the circus, he walked right smack into a telephone pole. His head was bleeding so badly that we went to the emergency room that day instead. That's awareness. Or think of it this way: being jarred into awareness is kind of like your mom smacking you on side the head and saying, "Snap out of it!" As adults, we learn to admonish ourselves ("G%&! @ IT! Arrgghh, stupid, wake up!") every time we crack an elbow or stub a toe. That is awareness.

The things that are supposed to help us, such as GPS or our Cell phones, tend to get us to turn off some of the best navigation systems we were born with, our instincts. Electronic devices are scientifically proven to contribute to addictive behavior resulting in an attitude of, "well, I can text and drive, it's the other person that cannot handle it." Which sounds very much like "well I can have a drink and drive, it's the other guy that can't handle it." This lack of awareness on how humans subconsciously train themselves to become unaware is at the heart of becoming more alert, alive and building a skill base that is strong enough to do the thing that is hardest to do in life, say no to yourself.

■ HABIT CHECK

Take a moment to become more aware of all the things you do that are not really what you want to do, such as getting up in the morning and mindlessly flipping on the computer to read emails. There is a good chance that you would rather reserve that early morning time for yourself to exercise or create. *Once you're aware that you have been inadvertently conditioning yourself to react,* you can switch back to living life the opposite way, which is proactively.

Awareness is listening to all five of your senses: sight, hearing, taste, touch, and smell—and most *especially your sixth, intuition, which is the ability to look inside yourself.* Awareness sits at the nexus of some of the biggest challenges in life. If we are not aware of threats, we similarly cannot be aware of opportunities.

Awareness applies to the discovery of new art. Literary agents, music agents, and scriptwriters are all looking for the new best thing. Those agents that are aware of new, undiscovered talent must trust their awareness skills to take a calculated risk on the unfamiliar artist. Awareness applies to investors. To seize financial opportunities in real estate, stocks, bonds, or retirement funds. Those of us who are looking to grow our wealth—and who isn't?—must be on the lookout for opportunities.

We might ask ourselves why some people are more successful than others, and often it is not that they are more fortunate, but that they are just more aware.

SHARPEN SKILLS HERE

MENTALLY AWARE

Be on the lookout for the wandering brain. Remaining aware and vigilant of our own mental wanderings and frailties is probably the hardest task of all. Mentally strong people do not waste time letting their minds wander off feeling sorry for themselves. They do not give away their power, do not shy away from change, do not waste energy on things they cannot control, and do not worry about pleasing others. One night on foot patrol, I felt my mind begin to wander, and I started to think to myself, "Um, self, you know what we have not thought of in a while? Monsters." And then I began to imagine dark, shadowy aliens on rooftops and proceeded to freak myself out. Our minds wander around all the time toward self-deprecating talk, old arguments, gossip, and complaints. Sometimes I feel like a rancher galloping out into the far reaches of the valley to gather up pieces of my wandering mind like stray livestock.

EMOTIONALLY AWARE

When people tell you to live in the moment, what they are saying is to be more aware, to be more present, more mindful. Not only because it means that you will enjoy life more, but because chances are that you will have fewer mishaps when you are paying attention. When you are feeling beat, blue, and badgered, your chances for letting in negative stress increases. Being emotionally run-down leads to impulsiveness and a tendency to react to every irritant. Plus, you become very difficult to work and live with. Letting your emotions get the best of you can create even deeper problems with attention, <u>depression,</u> and diet. Emotionally strong people take every opportunity to see the beautiful moments in life that are all too often drowned out by myriad anxiety and self-consciousness issues.

VISUALLY AWARE

Defensive drivers anticipate the things that can go wrong on the roadways. Constantly scanning, noticing what is going on five car lengths ahead, and taking evasive action keeps them from being involved in accidents. You can reduce your chances of colliding with other people and other similar situations by applying these same concepts. Before every incident are clues. Security specialist Gavin DeBecker calls them pre-incident indicators (PINs). Looking, scanning, and paying attention means that your face is not in your phone or looking down, that you quickly scan buildings as you enter them, and, before you sit down, that you take note of the exits and sit near them. The more aware you are, the less likely you are to miss small subtle movements, voice inflections, or gestures that could tip you off to something that would jeopardize your safety or well-being.

PHYSICALLY AWARE

I am a huge advocate of learning martial arts because just freaking people out with an aggressive look does not work. As James Brown said, "I might not know karate, but I know Kaa-razy." I studied jujitsu for seven years and learned how to move from my core. Centering oneself gives a person an incredible amount of physical control and self-discipline. How many people are not aware of their bodies as machines? They do not put in proper fuel, get proper rest, or exercise their bodies. As the old saying goes, without our health, we've got nothing. Most people I ran across in my line of work had problems with self-discipline, the ability to say no to themselves when it came to the bad stuff, and the inability to force themselves to do the good things. I admit that I was surprised to learn that when I began to study jujitsu, the art of self-discipline overshadowed the art of defense, because without one, you cannot have the other. Another bonus of staying physically fit is that you've mastered some level of confidence over your own body, which means that you are giving off positive vibes; repelling negative ones, making you less of a target for would-be predators. Also: be aware or in tune with other peoples' moods. If someone seems off, angry, or always complaining about being disrespected, be aware that they might be nearing snapping point. Get them help, be of help, or get away. Regarding physical safety, raising our awareness *requires us to listen and pay attention to our own bodies first, then to our surroundings.*

FINE-TUNING

Let's face it: being aware is just a better way to be. It means we can identify issues more quickly and formulate plans to deal with them. It requires listening and not just hearing; paying attention to finances and not just seeing them, listening to our bodies and caring for them, using inductive reasoning skills in all of our surroundings, and not reacting to what we see on the outside.

<u>My Favorite Quotes:</u> "To be thrown upon one's own resources is to be cast in the very lap of fortune." Ben Franklin

<u>My Favorite Author on Awareness:</u> *The Road Less Traveled*, by M. Scott Peck

———

ACTION PLAN: How can I become more aware?

_____

_____

_____

_____

_____

_____

_____

_____

_____

_____

CHAPTER 3

PEOPLE, THE DIFFICULT ONES

There tons of books on how to deal with difficult people, but simply accepting that they are around and in your personal space gives you a tremendous emotional advantage. I can tell you from personal experience that I was shocked and put on the back foot every time someone was an Ass to me. However, once I immersed myself in one of the few careers where you surround yourself with Jerks, it actually became easier. I can strategize now about how to deal with all the garden-varieties of Asses. You can do the same with a quick Google search.

Sometimes what makes dealing with the difficult, hard, is that we are completely clueless that there was a problem with them in the first place.

▉ MY STORY

Last summer, my elderly neighbor of ten years decided that he owned me. The driveway leading up to both our houses is on my property, but he considered himself an easement aficionado. He would saunter over daily and proceed to tell me where I could park, whether he liked my visiting family members or my new husband, where I should plant a tree, and the proper way to pet my pooch. I realized that he was becoming a little older and more territorial, and he had taken mental possession of me and my land. His whole family realized this change in his behavior and that it had become an issue, but like a fart in church, no one said anything. One morning while stuffing a spoon of Raisin Bran in my mouth, I looked up to find him staring in my dining room window. That was it. I reacted, went outside, and started yelling at him. I had lost all my trained self-control and had become this pathetic, slimy human, just reacting.

Looking back, I really should have been more proactive and strategized. I should have checked my emotions, gone over to his house, had a talk with his son (who lived with him) before I let myself lose control. After thinking about all this, I checked myself. His son and I are currently formulating a plan of action because he is still a difficult person, that will not change, only my reaction to him.

Today, I look at my little neighbor as a new challenge. Like you, my life is full and I don't need another burden, let alone a difficult person in my life, but that is what I have and many of you have at work, home or in your neighborhood. In this case, I have had to take a leadership role with my neighbor, suck up my emotions, and formulate a logical plan, stopping it from escalating.

■ HABIT CHECK

How many times have you been caught unaware that someone hated your guts. I know it was a shock, you go around doing all the right stuff and someone has it in for you, and then some years go by and it happens again and maybe again. Then surprisingly, you adopt a habit of hating yourself because somewhere, someone told us that bullies should not exist. That is not true, they do. History is filled with unhappy people who made life miserable for others; they will never go away, not at school, at work, or at the playground, not in a hundred years. So, stop the habit of admonishing yourself that you did something wrong, because it's a victim mindset and puts you at a disadvantage. Instead, get your power back by thinking strategically and tactically. Ask yourself, what is this person's problem? Research how others have handled this sort of person, and CALMLY implement your solution.

▨ SHARPEN SKILLS HERE

Only through strength and self-discipline will you be able to handle the difficult people in life.

Three ways to identify issues before they become problems.

1. Be proactive: Practice training yourself to be a proactive person rather than a reactive person. A great place to start is on your way to work. Did you ever notice how the horn which was designed as a warning device is now a tool to say F#$ You! This goads you to react and say F@!#$ you back. Retrain your brain not to respond, i.e react. Another way is to start habituating yourself to do your creative things first, early in the morning. Write, paint, or exercise: do the things that put you in a good mood, the things that are a *part of your agenda* and not someone else's.

2. Eliminate unnecessary emotions and feelings because they often lie to us.
3. Look at problems and issues as challenges to overcome, not obstacles. Attitude is everything.

First, examine: Define what the problem is. Based on what you know for sure, include what others know, and be honest about your attitude. Is it positive or negative? Next, formulate an approach. Accept that some problems will take more time; for others, the solution will be immediate.

Second, Plan: Be logical about the problem using a process of elimination, implement your plan of action, evaluate the results of your actions, reformulate if given new information, and try again.

LEADERSHIP

The idea of leadership has been romanticized, leading people to forget that leadership puts you right in front of difficult people; at church groups, within families, committees, at work or holding an office, you are now a target for criticism. But you can handle it because with the aforementioned tips, you are emotionally and physically prepared, you have strategized and are ready.

My Favorite Quotes: "Change your thoughts and you change your world," Norman Vincent Peale

My Favorite Author on Difficult People: How to Deal with Difficult People by Gill Hasson

———⟨⟩⟨⟩———

ACTION PLAN: List the issues with difficult people I am aware of right now that I need to address:

_____

_____

_____

_____

_____

_____

_____

_____

_____

_____

CHAPTER 4

TOOLS THAT COME IN HANDY

Imagine always being prepared. You're that guy or gal that always has emergency equipment in their car, home and office. It is completely refreshed and restocked with the most amazing gear, ready to respond to whatever life throws at you. I know, that's not always me either, life gets so complicated and often it's the best we can hope to get out the door and to work on time. The only emergency equipment we have is our wits.

MY STORY

Some years ago, a friend of mine, while in college, took a break from her studies and went for a drive. She would tell me later that she had noticed the car in the rearview mirror early on, but she had dismissed it, reasoning that the person driving that little green Toyota must have lived in the same neighborhood that she was visiting, and that there was nothing to worry about. Still, she felt uneasy. She admonished herself for worrying, telling herself that she was a whole twenty years old, a grown woman, and that she had to stop acting like a little girl. As she pulled over to go for a walk in an empty field, unbeknownst to her, the car following her did too. She recognized the large man who got out. He was a friend of a neighbor, and as he came up beside her, he started a conversation. He told her he was looking for his daughter's dog that had broken free from the yard and asked if she would help him find it. She agreed. Being in denial about the warning signs would cost her; she was raped at knifepoint and never finished college.

▧ HABIT CHECK

TOOL #1: INTUITION AND DENIAL

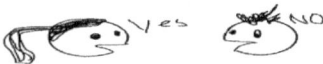

Are you a person that is in tune with their intuition or are you a person that regularly dismisses that inner voice?

My friend was in denial about what her feeling of uneasiness (intuition) was telling her. She did not want to believe or could not believe that she had so easily become the target of a criminal. So she comforted herself by making excuses for what her senses were telling her. Excuses such as, "This only happens to other people, maybe he is innocently going the same direction as me or perhaps he is on his way to go visit his sick mom in the hospital!" Who knows, the point is, that the sense of uneasy, changes the whole dynamic. Not wanting to confront or accept that a dangerous situation is about to happen, we humans often dismiss what is right there in front of our eyes and ears. Our intuition always has our best interests at heart and denial does not.

Does it look like a Duck?

Denial is a refusal to admit the truth when we either sense it or know it. An easy way to face facts is to do something cops call the duck test. The scenario goes something like this: if it looks like duck, swims like a duck, and quacks like a duck, then it is probably a duck. The test implies that a person can identify an unknown subject by observing that subject's habitual character. It is not a judgment, which is reserved for God alone, but an observation, imperative for our personal safety.

Beyond what we can see with our eyes, the duck test; intuition is the next best thing. When intuition relates to your immediate safety, you are right to trust it and get out of a bad situation, or from a person that you sense is not on the right side of good.

If you have time

When time is on your side, pause and incorporate some critical thought. Innocent people have been accused of wrongdoing based on poorly thought-out "feelings" about someone. If your intuition tells you there is something not right about someone and you have the luxury of time, put some critical thought into your analysis. Critical analysis should be skillfully conceptualizing, applying, analyzing, and evaluating information gathered from or generated by observational experience. Coming up with the truth of a situation or person requires reflection, reasoning, or communication if possible.

TOOL #2: TRUTH

Are you a person that knows how to find the truth, like how to properly research and get to the bottom of things?

Being able to identify truth gives you both physical and intellectual advantages. The truth must be tested and injected with more truth, which comes from many sources such as

- Your personal experience.
- History, or perspectives.
- *Sound research* from scholarly journals.

Note: Often the "latest" research is quickly debunked and replaced, so just keep that in mind. Finding truth also means factoring in gut feelings, because it is factually happening.

- Media Honesty- Opinion journalism is not truthful news. This sort of journalism can easily be spotted by the receiver when trigger phrases are used to create curiosity and fear.
- Angry reactions to Truth- Revealing and standing up for the truth means that our neighbors, friends, family, and coworkers might not like us anymore. But you must live with yourself and there is a much greater peace of mind when you live it despite lies others want you to believe.

One thing is for sure: to recognize truth, it must be lived. Seek the truth with everything you are, everything that you do, and everything you think. Only then will you be able to recognize truth.

A reliable way to find the truth is by applying the principles of reason:

- The most data is the best data.
- Remember the principle of noncontradiction: a thing must either be or not be.
- Objective evidence is not influenced by personal opinions in considering and representing facts.

TOOL #3: UNDERSTAND BASIC HUMAN BEHAVIOR

Do you have a clear understanding of human behavior? This is tremendously helpful when determining how people are likely to react to different situations giving you a tactical advantage on how to help or how to get out of the way.

All humans feel the following eight elements. They are known as pillars, and when one or more is knocked out, or begins to get knocked out, a person will seek balance to stabilize emotionally. When that person cannot regain balance alone, they will become defensive and he or she will lash out. This is the time to beware of others, or even yourself, who you know are struggling to seek a stabilizing person they can trust to help them through.

- We seek connection with others.
- We are saddened by loss and try to avoid it.
- We dislike rejection.
- We like recognition and attention.
- We dislike ridicule and embarrassment.
- We care what others think of us.
- We will do more to avoid pain than we will do to seek pleasure.
- We seek a degree of control over our lives.

TOOL #4: RECOGNIZE MANIPULATION

Sometimes only time on this planet will make you adept at spotting manipulative people. This is where working with trusted mentors will help you navigate the situations and people you are unsure about. The quicker you can spot them the better you can insulate your finances and self from injury.

The pity play is the number-one tip-off that you are being manipulated through appeals to your sympathy, to your goodness. Unscrupulous people like nothing better than having others feel sorry for them. This is an "in," and it makes good people put their guards down. Mentally strong people never, never, ever ask to be pitied.

TOOL #5: FORCED TEAMING AND OBLIGATION

Ask yourself if you are always the one to help but are also always the one who gets burned. Too much trusting is not a sign of niceness but naivety.

Forced Teaming is a technique used by both sales people and predators. If you are a sales person, then do not use this technique, instead create an environment where people want to buy from you. A fantastic book on this topic is called, "The little Red Book of Selling."

But for the sake of conversation so you understand what forced teaming is, here is an example, Time Shares. These sales people will often guilt you into a purchase with phrases such as, "if you cared about your family's peace and well-being you would buy into this time share." Caring people do care about their families and so do buy into the time share only to financially regret it later.

Another example would be a total stranger wanting and forcing him or herself on us offering to help us with a bag, package or our child. You see, it is the FORCEING that is the red flag. Not the simple offer to help. Pushy and unethical people use this strategy to enlist the "help" of another. It is a way of getting premature trust. It is a sophisticated manipulation that feigns a shared purpose.

Trust must be earned and should never be given away freely. *Remember, that he or she will make it difficult for you to walk away.*

TOOL #6: MANAGED RESPONSE TECHNIQUES

Not doing something about an issue, sometimes is doing something about an issue.

Norman Vincent Peal once said, "Part of the happiness of life consists not in fighting battles, but in avoiding them." A masterly retreat is in itself a victory." Ignoring a person that is bothering us may seem to be a sign of weakness, but I assure you very often it is not.

Engaging aggressors only gives them what they want. For whatever reason, they have become bored and chosen you as a target. Your best response is <u>a managed response. Managing your response involves controlling it and monitoring the problem.</u>

If the problem escalates, then you will quietly formulate a plan of action and do something about it, whether that is reporting it, laying out a plan to move away from the aggressor, or simply changing your phone number until that person moves on.

Tool #7: Pugilistic Intent

Are you aware that some people just like to fight? Knowing this is a huge advantage in avoiding needless confrontations that keep you from your goals. A modern term for these folks might be drama mama's.

There are varying degrees of these folks. One particular night I was called to respond to a bar fight where I came across Tex. He was a tall cowboy-looking sort of fellow, his face was bloody, he had a tooth knocked out and he was angry. I assumed he was angry because of the fight, but turned after I questioned him, he was mad at me! Yes me, for breaking up the fight, his fun.

Many people innocently stumble upon people who like to fight, this is where being a trained observer comes in handy because you can mitigate your interaction with these folks by first spotting them and then getting away from them. Again, this is not cowardice, so don't beat yourself up, it's called a MANAGED RESPONSE.

* Now, if a managed response or retreat is not possible from a pugilistic person you might try to kill em with kindness. When you hate your enemy, you confirm he is your enemy. But when you love your enemy you confuse and confound him, taking away the very energy that feeds his hatred.

There is a form of marital arts called Aikido. The idea of aikido is to absorb the aggressive energy of your opponent, moving with it, continually frustrating him until he comes to the point of realizing that fighting is useless. Creatively absorbing the aggression of your opponent, channeling it back against him or her, to show them the futility of violence is always an option. So, think about it, perhaps when someone insults you, send back a compliment instead of an insult. It will drive them nuts.

Tool # 8 How's my driving

This might seem odd to you but you can take stock of your whole life by being honest about what kind of driver you are.

Do you yield, to let others in? Do you cut other people off? Are you respectful of the slow lanes and the fast lanes? Do you scan the horizon looking for potential problems up ahead or use your rear-view mirror looking for potential speeders from behind, or are you distracted and never pay attention to any of that? Chances are the behaviors you demonstrate on the road are the behaviors you will live by in life, strictly because you are practicing them.

If you are a reactionary driver and not a proactive one you are creating a habit of being a reactionary person in every aspect of your life. You will be too late to respond to opportunities and obstacles will be in your face before you have time to respond. If, however you practice being proactive on the road it will spill out positively to other areas of your life. The brain seeks patterns and patterns you develop to be a proactive person manifest themselves so much more positively in your life than reactive habits and patterns.

Tool #9 Social Media

Cyber safety and security is relatively new and can be either complex or very basic depending on who is bothering you. Here are some of the cyber problems people face:

Social media bullying, stalking or targeting/Shopping Scams/Identity theft/Wi-Fi theft and safety on public sites/ Keeping stores and airports from tracking your movements/ Securing your smartphone or tablet/Creating strong passwords you will not forget/How to hide where you go online/ Keeping hackers out of your computer.

***********************SUPER IMPORTANT***********************

Be Honest with yourself regarding your use of Apps that use GPS to pinpoint where you are such as dating, acquaintance and friendship Apps. Although this decade is all about sharing everything about yourself, where you are, what you are doing and eating, it's not a smart or safe thing to share with people you do not know, really, really, really well!!

After researching many people who are professionals on the subject of computer safety I came up with one I really trust, check out www.Kommando.com/security

#10 SEEING WHAT YOU DO NOT SEE

There are more blind people in the world today than there was a decade ago! With our faces in our phones all the time, it has created an explosion of Inattention Blindness.

Now known as the Gorilla Blindness test, Inattention Blindness was studied by Daniel Simons, and can be viewed on YouTube by simply typing in Gorilla Blindness test. It is responsible for running over people in cross walks, driving into motorcycles, looking for car keys that are right there in our hands and not seeing a gorilla while playing basketball.

The reason that people fail to see what is right in front of them is because they are not focused on it, they are focused on something else. While some people seem to suffer from this more than others, or have what is known as a lower working memory capacity, not seeing what is right in front of you has happened to all of us at some point in our lives.

How do you stop it? Just be aware that it is a phenomenon that humans are susceptible; a sort of human trait, an achilleas heel, and can get worse when driven to distraction by electronic devices. If you know you're susceptible to it, recognize it and be extra mindful in all your daily activities. Honestly knowing something is a potential problem reminds you to be mindful.

#11 UNDERSTAND ADDICTIVE BEHAVIOR

Most everything can be addictive, it is controlling us, rather than us controlling it. Drugs, sex, gambling and smoking used to be the addictions that people recognized, but I think people do not accept and appreciate how electronics can also be just as addictive. The impulse and urge to pick up a phone and text while driving is responsible for hundreds of deaths and injuries across the United States each year. That quick hit of dopamine from the pleasure center of the brain is just too much for many to resist. Whether addiction is from nature or it is nurtured, it is best to be vigilant and guard against the things that could develop into a weakness. Addictions put you at a disadvantage since the care and feeding of them grows to an uncontrollable monster, putting itself before family, goals, faith, wealth and health.

■ SECRET TIP HERE

The trick to never becoming addicted to anything is to know your weaknesses and accept that life is not easy. If someone tells you that life should be easy, go the other way. Because it is precisely the struggle, the execution of action and engagement in life and involvement, that are, *the crucial elements of joy! Don't let people cheat you out of struggle, that is the secret place where strength comes from.*

—◦◦◦—

My Favorite Quotes: "Love all, trust a few, do wrong to none," William Shakespeare, *All's Well That Ends Well*

My Favorite Author on Life's Tools: *Emotional Intelligence*, by Daniel Goleman

—◦◦◦—

ACTION PLAN: Take inventory of the tools you possess both physically and mentally, get the facts and information you need to create action plans. Outlining a plan to deal with a difficult situation, a difficult person, bad job or bad finances will move you to action. Be honest about what kind of a driver you are, a personal accident history might reveal that you are a reactionary person. Move to being proactive in every single aspect of your life, start here, yes right here on this line right now.

_____

_____

_____

_____

_____

_____

_____

_____

_____

_____

CHAPTER 5

CHOICES WE FACE IN LIFE

▮ MY STORY

In my line of work, public service, there are people you never forget. Keith was one of them. Keith couldn't get it right from the time he was a kid. He thought going to church meant that he could ask God for a bike, steal it, and then ask for forgiveness. "No," his mom would tell him, "it doesn't work that way."

As a teenager, he mastered the art of weaseling out of things. He reasoned that the ability to do so differentiated people from all animals except the weasel. Once I witnessed his wife yelling at him, "You never look out for me."

Keith, always looking for a laugh, quipped, "Sure I do. When I see, you are coming, I run the other way." As I got to know him better, I began to understand why he kept ending up in jail. This most recent time was because he agreed to retrieve some personal items for a friend out of the friend's father's house—only he did it at night while sneaking through a window.

And every time he got confronted, he would shout, "Why don't they just leave me alone?" I couldn't take it anymore; I pulled him out of his cell and drew him a picture.

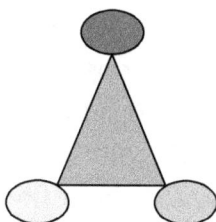

It's called the "crime triangle," a tool used in problem-solving. I took him aside and drew out the sides of the triangle, the victims, the offenders, and the location. These are the three elements of every crime situation. The crime triangle is used in problem-solving to foster a thorough analysis of crime patterns and how to take more effective action to reduce the harm that problems can cause.

Only in Keith's case, I wrote something different on each corner:

- **Proactive:** It means to create or control a situation by *causing* something to happen rather than responding to it after it has happened.
- It equals more **choices** in life.
- It creates a positive **rippling effect**, radiating outward into family and community.

■ HABIT CHECK

Getting more choices is like getting more wishes. Getting more choices means that we should *create situations* that give us more choices rather than responding to life.

Ask yourself when is the last time you invested in yourself so you could demand more out of your body, mind and resources? By Proactively choosing to take care of your spiritual, mental and physical needs first thing in the morning, you are giving yourself the physical and emotional reserves, you are going to need throughout the day.

Then get into your business with things like e-mails, which are other people's agendas to which you can then respond. Get in your car, go to work and that's when the nerve racking horn honking starts, people mad at the world and trying to suck you into it, but you are less likely to get pulled into the chaos because you chose to start out first thing in the morning refusing to react to these jerks.

It feels so awesome to choose to take the control back. I cannot tell you how many people I have counseled over the years with this one simple mind shift. In doing so, they *detach from others' agendas and toxic emotions.*

- The only person whose behavior you can control is your own. The rippling effects of that choice will be yours alone to deal with. A pebble of choice thrown into the pond causes a great rippling effect not only for us, but also for the others we bump into in this world. Poor choices ripple out negatively and outwardly, creating tidal waves of hurt and frustration that have little resemblance to the original pebble. One person really can make a difference for good or bad. Think about these situations and ask if some of these situations are your habits?

- The man who answers his cell phone while driving and causes accidents, leaving others to pick up the pieces of their lives after the wreckage.
- The parents who allow their children to rampage through a restaurant, while others who took the night off from their children in order to get a break, must now leave the restaurant in order to get any peace.
- The checks that deliberately get bounced at a local small business that force the business owner to cover payroll out of his or her personal savings.
- The manager who berates his employee, who then goes home depressed and takes it out on his or her child.

SHARPEN SKILLS HERE

CHOOSE TO CREATE A BETTER LIFE

People on the wrong side of life rarely choose loftier goals for themselves as in music, math, or a path of spiritual or physical betterment, they seem to be looking for the easy way out.

We do have a choice of what to follow *and when you follow beautiful ideas, things and people, it is less likely that you will expose yourself to dangerous and compromising situations.* Examples of people making these sorts of choices are everywhere.

Raised in the crime infested neighborhoods of Detroit, one young man decided to study science and listen to the masters of classical music. He eventually left the projects and went on to become a world-famous brain surgeon and recipient of the nation's highest civilian honor, the Presidential Medal of

Freedom, Dr.Benjamin Carson. He is not an outlier. I could find many that have practiced the discipline of looking up instead of down, but I will leave that choice to you, to seek and to find.

CHOOSE YOUR ATTITUDE

Your attitude is considered the control center of your life. And as such, you have control in choosing it. When we accept that life is difficult, we adjust our attitude to prepare for the difficulties. This is not to excuse those at work who randomly and flippantly attack you and say, "you need to change your attitude." This is different, and a personal assault. What I am talking about is you, your inner examination to relieve some of the burden of life. By taking on a more laid-back approach to the assaults that life throws at us, and not being so rigid, we are kinder to ourselves and more enjoyable to be around.

Unbelievably, there are a few who see us in a good mood, and want to knock it out of us. They are unhappy and it irritates them to see us happy. The only thing to be done in this situation is to identify, and either intercept and ask them why they want to destroy your good mood, or evade them and walk the other way.

Increasingly, it seems that many people lack communication skills. They make no effort to clean up their language. Blurting out unfiltered thoughts through memes, emails, posts or to someone's face has escalated out of control, creating a culture that has become mean and undisciplined, making it harder to have a positive attitude. The answer to this dilemma is the same. Are you a glass half full, or a glass half empty sort of a person? If you are an optimist then delete every negative person on your Facebook, seek out only positive news, and hang around only positive people that are being the change in the world they want to see and be. All this will have a profound effect on your attitude just as surely as exposing yourself to negative influences will.

CHOOSE TO SEEK 👀

When you *seek out the positive* it offsets the times you are forced to sit through the negatives. I remember the last time I was at a department committee meeting: Floyd Full-of-Himself burst through the door along with Randy Roughshod, their egos so large that I could almost visualize them being carried in wheelbarrows in front of them, as the men entered the room and parked their rusty carts next to themselves. They ran the meeting, egos in high gear, raising their voices over anyone that dared to speak. The head of the meeting let it continue unchecked and all this influenced my attitude. It did however make me mindful of the times that I might not be aware of how *I* might be coming off to other people, how my unchecked, persona could affect other people's attitudes to some degree. These are just questions to ask yourself, and in asking, you are already one step further to making the world a better place.

—◦◦◦—

<u>My Favorite Quotes:</u> "You cannot control what happens to you, but you can control your attitude toward what happens to you, and in that, you will be mastering change rather than allowing it to master you," Brian Tracy

<u>My Favorite Author on Choice:</u> *Choice Theory: A New Psychology of Personal Freedom*, by William Glassar, MD

———◦◦◦———

ACTION PLAN: Everyone does not always have a choice, sometimes life throws things at you that limits your choices. List the things you can control, and the things you do have choices about.

_____
_____
_____
_____
_____
_____
_____
_____
_____
_____

CHAPTER 6

MANNERS: AN INDICATOR OF SAFE OR SANE

Good manners never go out of style and will take you far; you cannot have a civil society without a sense of what is proper. There was a time not long ago that proper behavior was a sign of inner mental strength, wisdom, and superiority. Propriety had been a virtue for centuries. Today, media would have you think that egotistical aggression is a competitive advantage, or that saying what you feel and acting out is a sign of strength. Secretly, we all know that it is not. Civility makes a civilized world and begins with families then radiates outward into communities, the workplace, and the nation.

GOOD MANNERS MEAN NO POPO

A society that demonstrates that they can be civil to each other means there is less need for government to legislate our actions. Dictating all human behavior is enslavement. More laws require more judges, lawyers, and police, a process that results in a less civilized world. Propriety is a mainstay of what it means to be a civilized world. When people are nice to each other, there is less crime and people are filled with just a little more joy. Legislating manners does not mean people will behave properly, either; just think about it, Jaywalking, tailgating, booming music from a passing car, illegal dumping, driving while on the phone. There are laws against these, and yet people break them anyway, because they are ill-mannered and think that the laws don't apply to them or that they can get away with it. And, in fact, more laws create more of a pushback from people, they resent being over legislated, over governed, and over controlled. When societies control themselves, when people have manners and fewer laws are necessary.

SELF-RESTRAINT IS GOOD MANNERS

If you want to know who to allow into your inner circles, watch how they treat other people. A person that is rude or inconsiderate to others but not to you, is concealing their true personality, they have just not turned it on you yet.

Sincere good manners are the result of decorum and self-discipline, they are not shallow nor a tactic to get what you want. Good manners show respect and concern for the other.

Good manners are the practice of self-restraint; think about it, someone with a sense of what is proper has had to say, "no" to themselves on many occasions such as, too much food, too much recreation, and no to speaking when it could needlessly hurt someone. A well-mannered person is someone who has learned to control impulses. Good manners act as governors. They teach us to reign ourselves in from ourselves.

We all know it's wrong to gossip, but why? Because gossip is a form of bad manners it's stealing. By talking about other people behind their backs you are stealing their reputations, and we all know it's wrong to steal; someone's stuff, their money, their wife, or their life.

One final word on self-restraint, we are left with a conundrum, we live in a fast-paced world. The world tells us that if we do not seize upon an opportunity quickly and knock others out of the way, we risk losing out. But opportunity seeks out the generous, the ones who are self-restrained and offer to help others. They are offered far more opportunities than the unrestrained selfish person. Watch, look, and listen for people with good manners, be vigilant and don't let the fast-paced unrestrained world convince you that the world's rewards go to the desperate and unrestrained.

MY STORY

The hour was three o'clock in the afternoon, when I was called to slosh through the house of Trixie and her tribe. As I took the report of a stolen TV by an ex-boyfriend, I noticed a TV on in every room. "How could she possibly notice one was missing?" I thought. In the children's room, *Sesame Street* was on. That seemed okay, but then in Trixie's room, *Lifestyles of the Criminally Insane* was on, and *Jerry Springer* was on in the living room.

Many of the homes I entered had television on 24/7. Their T. V's were never off. With increasing frequency, the shows are negative. Shows about murder, adultery, broken families and addicted people. How can one ever break the cycle of negativity if that is all you feed yourself and your family?

We become what we put into our minds, what we surround ourselves with and what we intellectually eat.

Watching _How_ to do something rather than _how not to_ is a far better way of putting success patterns into your brain. Your eyes and consciousness now have a reference point from which to recognize and act on the positive things they see, hear, and smell. Positive Opportunities now become visible where before you might not have seen any. For example, have you ever been the unsuspecting witness to some great random act of kindness, seeing its ability to fill people with joy? Watch more joy, have more joy, become more joy!

PROPER PARENTING

Each generation brings forth the next bunch of barbarians that must be taught quickly before it is too late; what a civilized society is, and how to be a part of one. Functioning and flourishing nations only work when we are civil to one another. The whole concept of a free society is based on the idea that people can all be civil to one another, live with self-control and not act out willfully. Proper parenting passes the message of good manners and self-control on to their young from which we all benefit, and are truly grateful to those parents who take the time and effort to bring their children up in the way of good manners. I thank you and the world thanks you. It is one of the hardest jobs out there, but you are getting credit right here and now for taking the time to bring up a self-controlled child.

○ That's the way the cookie crumbles

When my children were young, I found myself challenged like all parents do. One sunny afternoon I gave my two-year-old a cookie to go with her milk, she accidentally dropped it on the floor where it split into two pieces. Without skipping a beat, she sighed and said, "Shit damn it." It was so stinking cute the way she parroted me in that helium-filled voice of hers. I practically burst out in laughter. Struggling to hold back fits, I told her that we cannot say things like that when we are discouraged. I turned my head so she wouldn't see this ridiculous smile on my face, as I struggled to stop laughing, took a deep breath, let out the air and faced her once again. "It's okay if you say the word darn, but the other word is not, and if you have ever heard me say that, I am sorry." You know that story is around twenty-five years old, but I still smile and crack up inside.

Something miraculous happens though, when you teach your children manners and deferral of gratification. They grow up and can self-discipline. They don't need Mom anymore to reign in their wild human behavior. We learn to control ourselves. We learn the deferral of self-gratification and don't act like cavemen in public. We are taught the art of being civilized; teaching this to the young is one of the most important jobs in the world, because it benefits us all to live in a civilized world.

My mom was a hat maker back in the day when hats were fashionable. She was the queen of the one minute lesson on manners, although she is gone now, these will live on generation after generation.

- Dress properly, and be presentable. The way you look shows that you respect yourself and in turn others will respect you. Pulling yourself together on the outside is likely to mean you are pulled together on the inside.
- Take care of your body and physical health with exercise, healthy food, and plenty of water. And it's okay to drink out of the hose.
- Take care of your mind; stay well-read, traveled, spiritually healthy, and educated; and think critically.
- If you're a guy, treat women with respect. If you're a gal, treat men with respect.
- Be grateful for what you have by volunteering. As the saying goes, to whom much is given, much is expected.
- Laugh, love, smile, and watch your ego.

―――∞∞∞―――

My Favorite Quotes: "Respect for ourselves guides our morals; respect for others guides our manners," Laurence Sterne

My Favorite Author on Propriety: *A Handbook on Good Manners for Children*, by Erasmus

―――∞∞∞―――

ACTION ITEM: List the classy people you know in your personal life and throughout history and today. It could be an actor a politician, a scientist, a humanitarian, someone that you think is a class act. Now list ways that you could pick up a manner or trait or two from them.

_____

_____

_____

_____

_____

_____

_____

_____

_____

_____

CHAPTER 7

FEAR, DIFFERENTIATING FROM GOOD AND BAD

Every time I hear someone pushing past fear I wonder if they are pushing past the good kind or the bad kind. The good kind keeps you safe, while the bad kind holds you back. Fear is a very misunderstood word for that reason. Many people misunderstand fear and worry. They run around giving a lot of advice that is misplaced or even harmful. Differentiating good fear that keeps us safe, from unreasonable fear that results in lost opportunities, is a personal soul-searching quest. The important thing is to not let fear control us; a mindful, proactive person evaluates the basis of his or her fear and then decides. Ask first, "Is my fear reasonable?"

MY STORY

One night I was on patrol and I had a run- in with a young woman that decided to conquer her fear. She found herself holed up in her house, too afraid to go out because of a recent mugging at the community college. The local evening news kept reporting similar stories over and over, making her fear grow. They used phrases and statements like "could be happening," "possible anarchy," and "stay tuned for more terrifying new developments." These trigger words used by media are designed to make us stay tuned in so that we watch more commercials and buy more stuff. The words they use are carefully selected and geared toward our amygdala's, the key fear center of the brain. Fear can be both a powerful motivator and immobilizer. Karen kissed her kitten, put down her cupcake, and walked out the door. She felt she needed to push past her fear of walking alone at night. I don't believe she did because it really is not safe to walk alone at night, our visibility is limited and there are fewer people out and about to help us if we run into trouble. It was not long before she sensed that she was being followed by a shadowy stranger who was approaching her faster and faster. Behind her, I walked faster too, constantly looking behind me, because I happened to be on foot patrol that night. Then I realized she was running from me. I yelled out who I was to her, but she did not believe me. In fear, she broke into a dead run until she tripped and face-planted on the asphalt, breaking her nose and fracturing her ankle.

People orient their lives according to their fears. They're afraid of this or that, of love, of dying, etc. When you live your life out of fear, you *turn inward*, which creates a downward spiral of more fear. There is confusion on what that fear is and what it is not. As with the word "love," there are many, many different meanings for fear. Emotional fear, phobic fear, success-related fear, and responsibility-related fear: the terms are thrown around in articles, in books, and on TV.

Media is one biggest purveyors of fear, the movie, "Taken" is presented on the premise of wanting to inform the public about a problem. It features a nice guy rescuing his daughter from sex traffickers, which is a good thing. They sell a lot of tickets to this fear based movie, however; the producers of the movie really don't give a rat's ass about the realities of sex slavery, if they did they would work to end pornography and the end of the exploitation of people.

The problem with shows that sell fear is that there must be a victim and an aggressor. Again, when we watch patterns (movies) of how not to do something rather than how to do it, humans deviate to patterns they have put into their brains, this bad response will be the one your mind reaches for in an emergency. The incredible thing about formulating a plan of action in your mind is that this positive response image is there ready when you need it, leaving you feeling positive, confident and empowered.

Mentally strong people live their lives not according to their fears, but to the love of truth, which gives them a sense of liberation, joy, and a sense of mission.

■ HABIT CHECK

Look at each kind of fear and examine your heart, see if you are feeding unreasonable fear the kind that keeps you from success or reasonable fear, the kind that keeps you safe.

FEAR DEFINED

An unpleasant emotion caused by the belief that someone or something is dangerous, likely to cause pain, or a threat.

AM I FEARFUL OF SUCCESS?

Fear of success is something that is understandable; wary of new responsibilities, doubts as to whether you are ready for them are natural and wise to consider. But, if you know you are moving in the right direction, put one foot in front of the other, be mindful of only the moment. The hyper-concentration on the here- and-now will push the nervousness away; not completely, but enough so you can move towards success.

Fear of failure, rejection and or looking bad are not good reasons to not do something. You will always wonder if you could have done it. There are plenty of people who look back at their lives and regret the things they did not do because of unreasonable fear. They were comfortable with the known, as we all are. When you try something new there is uncertainty that triggers fear. But who wants to stay the same everyday all day, in a world of comfort, in a world of the known and unchallenged? Not many.

When I went through the police academy I was very uncomfortable and nervous, I did not like those feelings, but I knew I was not going to die and so I pushed on. I felt elation at pushing myself to succeed even though it was not perfect. I was not the perfect shot, runner, boxer or report writer, but I finished. I was successful.

John 23: "Don't then live your life according to your fears, but live your life according to your dreams."

AM I FEARFUL OF BEING HARMED?

Fear as a premonition or intuition is good fear. Adrenalin kicking in is a good response that your body is getting ready for the fight. For instance, you may pull over when a man drives alongside of you, pointing at your car and pretending that something is wrong. It may not seem right to you, but against your intuition, you pull over anyway. Then you pause, you rethink where you are pulling over, you listen to yourself and decide instead to pull over to a well-lit, populated gas station and look the car over yourself. Many people afraid their car might explode have overridden their intuition and fallen for this trick. We have all heard the stories of the businessman who decided not to take a plane flight and then later learned that it crashed. But what about the stories we don't hear, like the person who did not sign that contract, move into an apartment complex, or take that job because something was just not right? Examine your fear for its validity.

There are many variations of fear of being harmed:

- **Paralyzed by fear:** Immobilizing fear freezes any action, either to move forward toward the opportunity or away from harm. This type of fear is a helpless stoppage of activity.
- **Chronic fear:** As a result of a process often started in childhood, these people still believe that something terrible is going to happen, even though they are older and wiser now. They can be pessimists, always thinking of the worst possible outcome. Hypersensitivity to perceived danger is also a sign of chronic fear and

a possible sign that this type of person might need a trauma recovery specialist.

- **Phobia:** This is an extreme or irrational fear of, or aversion to something. *Disagreeing with someone is not a phobia.*
- **Anxiety:** This is an emotion about future events, a feeling of worry, nervousness, or unease, typically about an imminent event or something with an uncertain outcome.
- **Anxiety and success:** Anxiety is a feeling about future events, such as test anxiety, pre-interview anxiety, and pre-speech jitters. It can also be the feeling you get when the boss wants to see you in the office. We do not feel anxious about the present or the past. If we want to achieve certain goals in the future, it's important to look at a little anxiety as a positive motivator.
- **Anxiety and harm:** Adrenaline is released in response to a stressful event to prepare the body for sudden action, fight, or flight. This is good, and you're going to need it to get out of the way of a speeding train or to defend yourself from an attacker. Embracing the idea that your body is helping you, puts your mind at ease about the adrenaline. Nerves are connected to the adrenal glands that trigger the secretion of adrenaline. This process happens relatively quickly, within two to three minutes of the stressful event being encountered.
- **Worry:** Our imaginations can be a fertile soil in which worry and anxiety grow from seeds to weeds. To some, worrying is a "magical amulet," according to *Emotional Intelligence* author Daniel Goleman. Some people feel it wards off danger. They truly believe that worrying about something will stop it from happening. When worrying, ask yourself, "How does this serve me?"

◼ SHARPEN SKILLS HERE

General George Patton is regarded as one of the most successful US field commanders of any war. Educated at West Point, he was trained to take calculated risks and not to jump headlong into foolish situations. Patton was once asked if he had ever experienced fear or uncertainty before going into the battlefield. He replied that he often experienced fear before every battle, but he added one important thing: "I never take counsel of my fears."

———◦◦◦———

My Favorite Quotes: "Good tactics can save even the worst strategy. Bad tactics will destroy even the best strategy," General George Patton

My Favorite Author on Fear: *The Gift of Fear*, by Gavin DeBecker

———◦◦◦———

ACTION ITEM: Take stock of your fears and list them here, on one side write the fears that are the ones that are keeping you safe and the fears that are keeping you from your dreams and goals.

_____

_____

_____

_____

_____

_____

_____

_____

_____

_____

CHAPTER 8

LOVE OF SELF AND LOVE FOR THE OTHER

Misguided love gets people into a lot of trouble! Vigilance is very, very important in this area and understanding what love is, and what love is not, is crucial.

■ MY STORY

When I met her, she was dressed in an all-red jumpsuit in a holding cell. Cookie had been convicted of a felony assault with a deadly weapon with the intent to commit murder; she had no prior criminal record. I was working in the jail at the time, and she was in my section of control, so I got to know her and her story. She told me that she had fallen for a guy her parents did not approve of, so she had run away from home with him. It was not long before she was pregnant with their second child. He had introduced her to the fantastic world of drugs, and they were off and running, directionless and with bills piling up. She had gotten a job selling cherries on the side

of the road and came home early one day to find her partner in bed with her aunt. She was so furious with both that
she took a baseball bat to them. Before you can say "happy
camper," she was spending the night at the county jail dressed
in a red jumpsuit. She told me that when she had originally
been arrested, she was sitting on a bench in a courtroom holding cell with a large woman next to her when she realized that
the two of them were the only ones dressed in red. She leaned
over to the woman and said, "How come we're in red, and
everybody else is in orange?"

"Well, honey, tell me what you did," said the large woman.
Cookie told her about how she caught her husband cheating
on her, to which the large woman said, "Oh, honey, now I
know it shouldn't be, your husband cheating on you and all,
but your cracking him with that baseball bat, uh, that's what's
called a fel-o-ny." Cookie told me that's when she got mad at
the Hallmark card company and all those magazines for selling her on this love crap!

"Funny thing," I told her, "you're the sixty-third woman I
have run across that's said the very same thing."

CRIME STATISTICS ON "LOVE"

Clearly humans have difficulty in choosing and knowing what
love is, what empathy is, and what caring is. A study by the
Department of Justice, Crime Statistics, reported that, among
murder victims, 16 percent were members of the defendant's
family. The remaining 64 percent were murdered by friends
or acquaintances, and only 20 percent were murdered by
strangers.

R.E.S.P.E.C.T.

Respect is the key word to understand in the love equation because love means allowing someone to come very, very close to you; your person, your finances, your children and your mind. Understanding that respect is a crucial part of love, will protect these things from anyone that would seek to use you or them. In a sometimes-lonely world people desperate to be loved make some really bad decisions on who they hand their heart over to. It's understandable, but not practical in the long run. There are so many other ways to be valued while you wait for the right person to come along.

True love wants what is best for the other person, while romantic love just wants the other person.

This one short saying is the best gauge for determining healthy love, both to evaluate others' feelings toward us and our feelings toward them. What you feel for another person should be all-encompassing. You care about that person's dreams, goals, and health. People who exhibit unhealthy love care only for themselves and how they can be made to feel happy. Knowing what love is keeps us from choosing a person who does not know how to love, or uses it against us. Power games are often played by those who pretend to love, but are only interested in serving themselves. When you demand answers to inconsistencies, a self-serving person often rejects the one demanding respect. That's okay, because rejection is protection. When we respect ourselves and demand nothing less of others, our attitude acts as an invisible force field, repelling those who would tear us down; those who would curse us because they cannot get in.

According to author Erich Fromm in *The Art of Loving*, "Love is a decision, it is a judgment, and it is a promise. Love is not a feeling. If love were only a feeling, then there would be no basis for the promise to love each other forever. A feeling comes and it may go." When you feel, yourself caring deeply for someone, you should question it. If your caring for that person does not involve a conscious decision, a choice based on good, sound judgment, how can that feeling possibly last forever?

LOVE SELLS WELL

One of the most lucrative things to sell is not a thing at all, but love. Romantic love sells us millions of dollars' worth of makeup, perfume, dating sites, sexy clothes, shoes, and cars to attract our perfect mates—and yes, there is a hallmark card for all of it. When we do not have a person in our lives to love us, there are plenty of commercials and ads that make us feel left out, because we don't have that one person. I beg you to consider one thing: that love comes in many forms. There are plenty of ways to be loved by others; volunteering, a child's love, the love of an elderly person, the love from your parent or really good friend. Often times it is really not the love of a partner we are seeking. What we are seeking is relevance. Victor Frankle had it right when he said that there are plenty of people that live without being loved and without sex, *but what no one can live without is relevance.* Perhaps what you need is to be more relevant, than to find a date.

When looking for genuine love be vigilant and look for genuineness.

◼ HABIT CHECK

SMILING

Are you a sucker for a great smile?

Smiles are great. Mother Teresa said, "Let us always meet each other with smile, for the smile is the beginning of love." I agree, but *a smile* does not equate goodness, and neither does *being nice.* It is not my intention to split hairs regarding words, but too often we hear statements like this: "He was such a nice guy. Who would have thunk he would have shot all those people!" We must reexamine our flippant use of the word "nice" and the way we equate it with smiling a lot to mean a person is safe. The word "goodness" would be a better indicator of the content of someone's character. Ask yourself, "Is this person a *good person?*" How does this person treat people from whom he will not benefit? Is he or she honest, trustworthy, and just?"

FRIENDS AND ACQUAINTANCES

Do you know what true friendship looks like?

According to Facebook, the average number of "friends" people have on the site is 120. The word "friend" is tossed about these days like a ball at the beach; most people are acquaintances and do not have our best interests at heart. In fact, women posing as friends, encouraging their girlfriends to just get laid to solve all her problems, get more women in trouble than men do. According to the website Hooking Up Smart, on the college dating scene:

"Many young women in college want a relation-ship, not a random hookup. It's not surprising that many frustrated young women wind up dropping their drawers while drunk, hoping for the best, just to be included, part of the scene, having a normal college experience."

Honestly, in your entire life you will be able to count on one hand your true friends. Maybe even on one finger, sadly. But those are the friends you need to cherish and take care of and not use the word "friend" so loosely. Maybe these few friends you need to call today and tell them how valuable and loved they are. Because, in the end, I would rather be with that one friend than a whole room full of people who are just passing time.

During my years in law enforcement I ran into more peo-ple who got into trouble because of their "friendships" than those who didn't, which made me realize that people are *not really sure what a good friend is*. The excuses for getting arrested ranged somewhere between "It's my friend's bag of weed" to "My friend's boyfriend made me do it." These excuses made me compile a list to identify what I believe are some of the qualities to look for in a friend.

A true friend:

- Should help you to become the *best* version of yourself
- Is not morally relative, but strong
- Won't put you down or deliberately hurt your feelings
- Is kind, loyal, and has respect for you
- Is trustworthy and willing to tell you the truth, even when it's hard
- Is someone who laughs genuinely and not at the expense of others

—◦◦◦—

My Favorite Quotes: "When the wrong people leave your life, the right things start to happen," Zig Zigglar

My Favorite Author on Relationships: *The Art of Loving,* by Erich Fromm

—◦◦◦—

▨ SHARPEN SKILLS HERE

Think and list all the loves of your life, your mom, dad, sister, brother, teacher, minister, grandma, boyfriend, girlfriend and yes, even your dog. As you write, note the direction their love is coming from. Is it conditional or unconditional, built on respect or just one-sided? Maybe even ask yourself how they see you, is there room for improvement in all these relationships.

_____

_____

_____

_____

_____

_____

_____

_____

_____

_____

CHAPTER 9

MONEY, IT COMES IN HANDY

I was about thirty years old when the penny dropped for me. I finally understood how money worked; that people who have it look at their dollars differently than those that don't have it. I learned that a person who has money will look at each dollar and think about how they can make more dollars with it, while those that do not have dollars look at a dollar and think, "how can I spend this?" This simple yet crucial mind shift is monumental in getting and keeping and growing wealth. Because wealth is simply the exhaust fumes of a very energetic and creative mind like this joke represents.

A man enters a bank and asks for a loan of $2,000 for a trip to Europe. The loan officer asks for collateral, so the man points to his Rolls Royce parked outside. The bank takes the keys to the car and parks it in its underground parking lot. The man returns from his vacation and repays the $2,000, plus a minimal amount of interest (less than $20). The loan officer says, "Sir, while you were away, we found out that you're a millionaire. Why did you need to borrow such a small sum of money?"

The man replies, "I didn't. Where else in New York City could I park my Rolls Royce for two weeks for less than $20?"

It's a clever joke, maybe not entirely ethical, but funny. It does however, illustrate financial moxie. Most of the people I ran across in my line of work were not financially well-off, and many told me they simply did not know how to be, that they had no clue how money operated. It is a crime that public schools do not educate people on how to create the very thing that will help to sustain them and their families. Money is the lifeblood of existence. Without it we cannot provide electricity to run our homes, or buy gas for our cars. But, of late, it has gotten some bad press by being equated to greed and evidence of an uncaring society. This is certainly not the case. How else can we love our families other than to provide for them? Money is simply the exhaust fumes of pure hard work. There are some people who, if you gave them an ax and left them alone in a forest, would have the whole thing chopped down in a week because they are so driven.

The lack of financial literacy left me annoyed both at a public-school system that did not teach it and at a criminal justice system that is designed to financially penalize first, then incarcerate, leaving many locked into the "system" in a perpetual loop. Clearly, money is a problem that needs to be understood and respected.

LEARNING ABOUT MONEY

Learning how to make money, keep money, and make it grow will be a lifelong endeavor for most people. But there is good news because there are some basics. With a slow, steady approach, and not some get-rich-quick-scheme, you can build a nice empire. I want you to have more money, because more money gives you more choices, more freedom, more ways to take care of yourself and the ones you love. There are only a few people that understand the basics of money and how to educate others about it. Since there are too many bad books on money I will give you the name of one good one, *Thou Shall Prosper: The Ten Commandments for Making Money*, Rabbi Daniel Lapin. I love this first part of his book, it really sums up a lot of things.

> "Some valuable skills are transferred in many disciplines of life and, not surprisingly, learning how to increase your ability to make money and produce wealth is one of them. Learning how to make money suffuses every aspect of your existence, it sometimes turns things on their heads....Very rarely does a person accumulate wealth without acquiring social skills."

The second advisor I recommend is Dave Ramsey. You can find him on the radio or buy one of many of his books.

■ HABIT CHECK

Have an abundance mindset, it will leave you calmer and inspired to go chase that dollar and not begrudge it with a poverty mindset.

- **A poverty mentality** tells people that there is a lack in life in which opportunities are few and far between. This sort of thinking can be quite painful and create a lot of fear, depression, and anxiety.
- **An abundance mentality** tells people that there are plenty of opportunities for everyone, so they can just relax. The focus is directed on what is available, what the possibilities are, and how to appreciate and be grateful for who is in your life, and the resources that you do have available to you. *Not surprisingly, an abundance mindset requires one to be proactive, organized, and ready to seize opportunities.* But abundance requires you to both give back time to other people of a similar mindset in order to share that mindset, and to share the wealth that is left in your wake of positive productivity.

Change your attitude about money:

- Look at dollars as employees and not something to spend. Think first, "How can I make this dollar work for me?"
- Look for financial opportunities outside of what is obvious. The best and most lucrative financial opportunities are often never advertised. Finding them requires looking and listening—Vigilance!
- Network with other people that are financially literate.
- Accept that you will make mistakes. Don't seek perfection.
- Learn to foretell the future, look for trends, and raise your level of awareness.
- Teach family members to invest in themselves and their education. In order, be a good steward of money, you must first respect yourself.
- Be and autodidact and expand your own education goals.

———ᴏᴠᴏ———

<u>My Favorite Quotes:</u> "First, have a definite, clear practical ideal: a goal, an objective. Second, have the necessary means to achieve your ends: wisdom, money, materials, and methods. Third, adjust all your means to that end," Aristotle

<u>My Favorite Author on Finance:</u> *Thou Shall Prosper: Ten Commandments for Making Money*, by Rabbi Daniel Lapin

———ᴏᴠᴏ———

■ SHARPEN SKILLS HERE

I know I hate this too, but you gotta do it, really. Write out your finances and project where you are versus where you need to get. We all want to be rich, but break it down, take small steps and make a time line, then work it. You won't believe how empowering this is to have an action plan.

_____

_____

_____

_____

_____

_____

_____

_____

_____

CHAPTER 10

WORK A FOUR-LETTER WORD

The millions of people that earn their living serving others astounds me; hospitals, food service, jails and prisons, senior care, day care. If you are one of these people you can never get paid enough, and when difficult people make your job even harder, that is where I want to make your life easier.

▉ MY STORY

I worked with this guy once who hated to see anyone in a good mood, so he went out of his way to ruin it. His name was Nick.

He was a proper civil servant. He came in to work each day flat-footed and shuffling, miserable to be there. His knees buckled so that his hands dragged on the ground, making him look like some sort of gorilla. His briefcase was clutched in one hand, coffee mug in the other, and he wore a face so sour that it could curdle milk. Our faces lined up in a window of the sheriff's department, dreading when the sergeant would clock in for duty. The only thing we did not like more than him was each other. The toxic work environment seemed hopeless with a leader who was not much of a leader.

If not now, then at some point in your life you will have an experience with this sort of work environment. If you never have, then you have either reached the end of your work life and are lucky or dead. For the rest of us, we have had to go along to get along. You know the type of people we are talking about, the ones who pretend to be busy at the Xerox machine, or the ones who feign an injury and must go home every other day, forcing you to cover their shift. Or, how about the ones who use special holidays. Each week they are observing a newly-declared religion to be excused from something. You don't say anything and try to get along, so you go along with the practical joker who puts tomato juice in the break room refrigerator, labeling it pig's blood and swearing you to silence, even though you think it's a stupid practical joke.

■ HABIT CHECK

DON'T BE BLINDSIDED AT WORK, KNOW THE MOST COMMON OBSTACLES

⏻ **Power seekers:**

Then there are those who struggle for power. Humans have been at this for centuries, dating back to the aristocratic court that formed itself around the person in power, the king, or the leader. Courtiers served their masters, but if one seemed to fawn over the master too much, the other courtiers would notice, get jealous, and act against that courtier. Today, we might call this person a brownnoser and expect other employees to begin the sabotage.

The term "Going Postal," was coined after more than one United States postal worker lashed out killing co-workers spawning countless research papers as to why. But no paper was really needed, a crushing workplace filled with power seekers and leadership indifferent to the needs of its employees is an environment to be on the lookout for. If you are in one, think of ways to get a different job. If you are in an interview, make sure you interview the interviewer as well.

BOSSES: Accept that there will be bad bosses. According to Jim Collins, author of *Good to Great*, people do not leave bad jobs. They leave bad bosses. Managers often either do not see or do not want to see power plays in their own office. Being vigilant has everything to do with accepting facts and then planning. In this case, the fact is that there will be jobs that you must take legal action against or that you might have to leave. Saving money for when this happens is a proactive step in the right direction.

DIFFICULT Co- Workers: Life is difficult. People are difficult. Understand that we are born into a world at war. Opting out of the game will only leave you powerless and miserable. Instead of bemoaning and struggling against the inevitable, it is far better to understand it, change the way you look at it, and either lay out a plan to change it, deal with it or use a managed response technique and choose to step away and not engage.

EMOTIONS at Work: Master your emotions. Emotions cloud reason. If you cannot see the situation clearly, you cannot prepare for and respond to it with any degree of control.

ANGER at Work: Anger is the most destructive of emotional responses, it clouds your vision the most. It has a ripple effect that invariably makes the situation less controllable, and it heightens your enemy's resolve.

EXAMINE Work History: Look to the past and the mistakes you have made in dealing with people who have abused power. Try to educate yourself where you went wrong. Reexamine the situation, detach emotionally from it, analyze it, and then break the pattern.

MASKS People wear at Work: People wear masks to survive or manipulate. What separates humans from animals is our ability to lie and deceive. Power requires the ability to play with appearance, to have a bag full of deceptive tricks. Odysseus, for instance, was judged by his ability to rival the craftiness of the gods, stealing some of their divine power by matching them in wits and deception.

Escape Plan: If you find yourself in a difficult and unbearable work situation be financially prepared. Money is a tool. Making money, saving it, and investing it gives us more options in life. Make a very personal choice by deciding either to stay and fight or to leave. In either case, laying out a plan and making a goal are greatly empowering. Being aware of power games being played helps you to avert workplace disasters. Having enough money saved up for the inevitable battles in life is never a bad idea.

▓ SHARPEN SKILLS HERE

My Favorite Quotes: "True...there is no 'I' in 'team,' but there is a 'U' in 'suck,'" author unknown

My Favorite Authors on Work: *Good to Great: Why Some Companies Make the Leap...and Others Don't*, by Jim Collins, and *The No Asshole Rule*, by Robert Sutton, PhD

—◦◊◦—

ACTION PLAN: A dream job can turn into a work nightmare fast, when you are looking for a job, think of the people you like to work with rather than the actual work. I once knew a very happy man who was a septic pump operator! The world needs all sorts of workers, every job is valuable. List the places you would like to work or perhaps the entrepreneurial endeavor you would like to start.

_____

_____

_____

_____

_____

_____

_____

CHAPTER 11

IMMEDIATE ACTION REQUIRED

Nothing will stop you from reaching your goals faster than to run into a character-flawed individual. This is beyond a difficult person, this is a dangerous person, vicious killers and predators. This is not to be confused with simple goofiness because we have all had mental wanderings. You know that inner voice that you're always fighting with, the one side that says you're awesome one minute and a piece of shit the next? That is not what I am talking about, that is normal. Most normal humans struggle with their dark side and good side but manage to get the dark side under control. It is a human condition that the American Indians told stories about.

"The Parable of The Two Wolves."

A young grandson asks his grandfather why some people are evil and some are good. The grandfather tells his young grandson that each human being is born with two wolves that sit atop each shoulder and depending which wolf the human feeds, will determine his character.

Our modern world is quick to label everyone as not "normal," that we all have some sort of mental problems. We are warned and admonished not to judge others, to turn off your judgment switch and accept everything. If the world really operated this way, Police would not be able to determine suspicious behavior. If there was no normal, a doctor would not be able to diagnose sickness. If there was no gauge, no bar, the Olympics would be obsolete since no one would be allowed to say what a perfect performance was. So, make judgments and observations, your life depends on it.

Vicious - People who look normal, but are character-flawed can take time to spot. They are people that all the CSI shows are about. They are the ones who exploit others. They are back-stabbers, manipulators, liars, cheaters, and can be violent. They indoctrinate and brain wash. They come in every different profession, size, sex, age and color. It is because of the variety of crazy out there that it is difficult to spot the subtle differences in his or her warped philosophy of life. Are they mentally ill? Perhaps; but it does not make a difference to you when you are attempting to live your life unmolested and move out of their path.

According to Harvard psychologist Martha Stout, due to society's increased emphasis on the self, narcissism, and an increase in those who have no empathy for others, sociopathic behavior is on the rise. She describes sociopaths as people that have *"the ability to hide their evil outwardly. They look and act not like the obvious villains we meet in the movies, but like ordinary folks we meet every day, in fact even nicer, smarter, and more attractive."*

LOOK FOR FACTS DON'T DWELL

When reading about the latest act of violence, search for patterns that would indicate to you a way to identify problem people in your world. Don't dwell on its negativity, just glean and don't worry about political correctness. When it comes time to reporting someone you suspect could be violent, political correctness is the worst construct for our personal safety.

■ MY STORY

The alleged gunman in Friday night's shooting at the University of California Santa Barbara campus also stabbed his three roommates in their home before beginning his rampage, Santa Barbara County Sheriff Bill Brown told reporters Saturday night. "It was a pretty horrific crime scene" at the apartment....

> Rodger engaged police in a shootout before he died from...a self-inflicted gunshot wound.
>
> Rodger was reportedly under psychiatric care and "diagnosed with 'highly functional Asperger's syndrome' as a child," the BBC reported....

Washington Post reporter Phillip Bump said police told him they investigated Rodger <u>but concluded he was not dangerous!!</u>

▪ HABIT CHECK

TAP INTO YOUR INTUITION DAILY

A little knowledge and our trusty instincts serve us well when separating the good guys from the bad guys. George Simon Jr., PhD, author of *In Sheep's Clothing*, states:

> "All character-disordered individuals, especially aggressive personalities use a variety of mental behaviors and interpersonal maneuvers to help ensure they get what they want. This accomplishes a few things; first, it conceals aggressive intent; second, their use puts others on the defensive; third, their habitual use reinforces the user's dysfunctional, but preferred way of dealing with the world; lastly because most people don't know how to correctly interpret these behaviors, they are effective tools to exploit, manipulate, abuse and control others."

DO YOU QUESTION IF IT IS ON PURPOSE?

This brings us to an equitable question: is evil a mental illness, or is evil deliberate and unforgivable? This is only an important question because so many excuse bad or mentally ill behavior, and think it is kind to do this, rather than what would really be kind is to get this person help.

Where does the line between mental illness and evil begin and end? As Aristotle maintained, *"Being evil portends a persistent habit of doing bad things."* Today, organic mental disorders are known as "no-fault diseases." According to the National Alliance of Mental Illness, it means that the individual was a product of his or her environment. For example, being abused as a child was not a person's fault, and consequently neither is his or her bad behavior. This sort of categorizing is best left to psychologists and lawyers who must sort it all out after an incident and not something our safety needs concern itself with.

PRESCRIPTION DRUG USE ON THE RISE:

Could it possibly be true that, according to the AMA, one in five Americans is mentally unstable? Or could it possibly be a way to excuse bad behavior or to sell more medication? Medication has its place when properly prescribed, but when it is not, the effects are felt by more than just the person taking it. According to Drug Watch, although once considered a taboo in American culture, antidepressants like Prozac have become the most prescribed drugs in the country. Today, about a dozen SSRIs [Selective Serotonin reuptake inhibitors] are prescribed, including Paxil, Zoloft, and Prozac....SSRIs are prescribed to treat depression, anxiety disorders, panic attacks, and personality disorders....SSRIs can interact with other drugs or supplements in negative or positive ways. SSRIs have several common side effects, including sexual side effects.... Fatigue, weight loss, apathy, insomnia, headaches, and pupil dilation are among the other most frequently reported side effects....SSRIs can also cause suicidal thoughts and actions, especially in teenagers.

Yet, the disturbing trend is to excuse every egregious behavior with a label. Don't excuse bad behavior, identify it and decide how you are going to handle it.

■ SHARPEN SKILLS HERE

One of my favorite bestselling authors, Scott Peck, of "*The Road Less Traveled*," was asked many times by his patients, "Doctor, why is there so much evil in the world?" His response:

> "*If we seriously think about it, it probably makes more sense to assume this, a naturally evil world that has somehow been mysteriously 'contaminated' by goodness, rather than the other way around. The mystery of goodness is even greater than the mystery of evil.*"

—⟪⟫—

My Favorite Quotes: "Never did I realize that mental illness could have the aspect of power, power! Think of it: perhaps the more insane a man is, the more powerful he could become." *One Flew Over the Cuckoo's Nest*

My Favorite Authors on Deviant Behavior: *The Sociopath Next Door*, by Martha Stout, PhD, and *In Sheep's Clothing*, by George Simon, Jr.

—⟪⟫—

ACTION ITEM: List places or situations that you feel are reasonable risks, like a gas station you frequent, the laundromat, the bank you go to, the park you take your dog to, or the gym you frequent. Ask yourself if there is a person that you come into contact with that makes your intuition scream, if so, chances are you are encountering a character-flawed individual that poses risks. Then list what you are going to do about it, either not go to those places, scan the area before you pull up to it, or take a buddy.

_____

_____

_____

_____

_____

_____

_____

_____

_____

_____

CHAPTER 12

WISDOM, THE QUALITY OF HAVING, KNOWLEDGE EXPERIENCE AND GOOD JUDGMENT

There is a single cartoon I came across in the newspaper over thirty years ago, and I remember it vividly because it sums up life. It looks something like this: a picture of a very old bearded man who represents God, stirring this giant caldron. In the caldron are animals, people, and the Earth. Above, he shakes a jar of seasoning labeled "Jerks." Under the cartoon, it reads: **"Just to make it interesting"**

KNOWLEDGE: THE TRUE

The preceding chapters are some of the most common obstacles I saw people face in my years of law enforcement. Knowledge is powerful because you cannot operate without information. Having it means you have greater choices, however, combined with experience and sound judgment the possibilities are greatly enhanced.

To know who you are, to be set firmly on a foundation of clarity and truth, is a fantastic way from which to pivot your whole life. I am lucky, I came from a very large family, my parents taught us the importance of lifelong learning, and so I have always enjoyed exploring and growing in as many ways as I can. I put a high premium on being a well-rounded individual with a vibrant mental life, spiritual life and physical life, so it has been important to me to find interests that fulfill me in all those areas. Martial arts, painting, writing, growing a small vineyard, studying entrepreneurship and volunteering are all interests that have stuck with me. As I grow I am sure there will be plenty more.

EXPERIENCE: THE GOOD

As you walk this journey called life, look for opportunities to engage the culture and share your faith in the life you live, in who you are and in your work. Your relationships are far more than *what you do* for work. So many people I meet have this idea that they have some great important work to do that will change the world. In the process of pursuing that, many of them end up passing by the daily opportunities to affect the people around them in positive ways. They miss the opportunities to demonstrate to neighbors, coworkers and friends a life of integrity, love and self-sacrifice. Who we are and how we live our lives is far more important than the "what" of our lives.

Wisdom: The Beautiful

We miss valuable insights when we only look at knowledge and experience by themselves, as if life is nothing but the scientific method: Question, test, analyze results etc., by doing so we restrict our growth as in the parable of the Cave, and miss out on some beautiful things beyond.

As you experience life, you will see the bad and experience bad, but it is imperative that you not dwell in this poison, because you will surely see more good. So, stay vigilant and expose yourself to the things and people that remind you of the beautiful, of all the things you have forgotten. And then share them in a beautiful way that makes people grateful for all the small things in life. By sharing the beautiful things in this world, you will attract more truth, goodness and beauty. And I would maintain that thanks are the highest form of thought, and that gratitude is happiness doubled by wonder.

—◦◦◦—

**You know what is best for you, always be a
TEAM *of* ONE**

Truth, always look for it, know how to use the principles of reason and flesh it out.

Emotion, don't let them drive the car but don't throw them in the trunk either

Awareness, take stock of items and situations around you

Move, be prepared to make a decision once you have all the facts, move.

Organized people are more efficient, be organized with everything!

Nutrition, eat healthy, exercise healthy, watch healthy, be healthy

Experience, along with Knowledge executed with good judgment equals wisdom. Throw a pebble in the pond and share your wisdom and be grateful.

▨ SHARPEN SKILLS HERE

My Favorite Quote: "A pessimist is one who makes difficulties of his opportunities; an optimist is one who makes opportunities of his difficulties," Harry Truman

My Favorite Author on Rippling Effects: *How to Win Friends and Influence People*, by Dale Carnegie

—⌇⌇⌇—

Experience, knowledge and good judgment; think of all the times in your life you either stopped something bad from happening because of this combination or created something fantastic because of this combination.

_____

_____

_____

_____

_____

_____

_____

_____

_____

EPILOGUE

Thirty years later after my first dog fiasco, I drove to the Animal Shelter and walked up and down the aisles of cages looking for a dog that resonated with me. Past Chihuahuas and Pit Bulls I found a small shepherd mix with a docked tail. She was a confident and playful four-month-old, young enough to bond with me and old enough to go on walks. I named her Sallie and took her home, only this time, I hired a personal dog trainer. He taught me about dog dominance, that it is in a dog's nature to attempt to control. That is why you see so many owners being drug by their dogs to the park rather than walking calmly side by side. What you see is not a mutual admiration society but a relationship where the dog is asserting control. Dogs respond well to tough love, they get peace and pleasure in knowing you are in control, that there is order and respect.

Because Sallie is an intelligent and high energy dog, I enrolled her in dog Agility competitions where she does well, when she is not off chasing a butterfly. She has taught me the importance of staying vigilant to any deviation she shows of trying to dominate me. She has shown me that an ounce of prevention is worth a pound of cure, and that no matter how inconvenient, I stop bad behavior when I see it. _This is vigilance to her training routine_ and I avoid having to fix problems later, this way I can truly enjoy experiencing the perfect dog of my dreams.

- I would like to thank the many vigilant peace officers whom I have known over the years and those that I do not know for being a positive change in the world. For working side by side with me, for sharing these stories with me, and sharing their skills in communities everywhere. Thank you for helping and serving and protecting tirelessly on a daily basis.

REFERENCES

Carnegie, Dale. 1998. *How to Win Friends and Influence people.* New York: Pocket Books.

Collins, Jim. 2001. *Good to Great: Why Some Companies Make the Leap...and Others Don't.* New York: Harper Business.

DeBecker, Gavin. 1999. *The Gift of Fear.* New York: Dell.

Erasmus, Desiderius. 2011. *A Handbook on Good Manners for Children.* Australia: Preface Digital.

Fromm, Eric. 2006. *The Art of Loving.* New York: Harper Perennial Modern Classics. 15th Anniversary Edition.

Glassar, William, MD. 1999. *Choice Theory: A New Psychology of Personal Freedom.* India: Harper Collins Publishers.

Goleman, Daniel. 2005. *Emotional Intelligence.* New York: Bantam Books. 10th Anniversary Edition.

Lapin, Daniel. 2009. *Thou Shall Prosper, Ten Commandments for Making Money.* New York: Wiley. 2nd Edition.

Maxwell, John C. 2007. *The 21 Irrefutable Laws of Leadership.* Nashville: Thomas Nelson; Revised & Updated Edition.

Peck, Scott, MD. 1988. *The Road Less Traveled.* New York: Touchstone.

Simon, George, Jr., PhD. 2010. *In Sheep's Clothing.* Michigan: Parkhurst Brothers Publishers Inc; First Edition, 2nd Edition.

Stout, Martha, PhD. 2006. *The Sociopath Next Door: The Ruthless Versus the Rest of Us.* New York: Broadway Books.

Sutton, Robert, PhD. 2007. *The No Asshole Rule.* New York: Hachette.

www.ingramcontent.com/pod-product-compliance
Lightning Source LLC
LaVergne TN
LVHW051812080426
835513LV00017B/1925